THE TRUMP PRESIDENCY

A Pastoral Perspective

Answers to the **Top 10 Questions** About Faith, Leadership, and Public Life in the Trump Era

LORENZO SEWELL

REVIVAL HOUSE
PUBLISHING

For permissions, contact the publisher at
publisher@revivalmagazine.global

First paperback edition: January 2026

Edited by Amanda Cheatwood
Cover and interior design by Amanda Cheatwood

Printed in the United States of America.

Published by
Revival House Publishing LLC
30 N Gould Street, STE R
Sheridan, WY 82801

ISBNs
Paperback: 979-8-9944266-0-9
Hardcover: 979-8-9944266-1-6
eBook: 979-8-9944266-2-3
Audiobook: 979-8-9944266-3-0

Contents

Acknowledgments

First, I give honor to God, the One who saved me, changed me, and sustained me. If there is any good in these pages, it is because of Him.

To my wife, Molly, thank you for loving me with strength and patience. Thank you for carrying weight with me, not just cheering from a distance. You have been my covering, my peace, and my reminder to stay anchored when the noise gets loud.

To my children, Isabella, Elijah, and Naomi, you are my joy and my motivation. Everything I do is not just about today. It is about the world you are growing up in. I love you more than you will ever understand, and I am always going to fight for your future.

To 180 Church, thank you for being family. Thank you for believing that Jesus still changes lives, still restores cities, and still sends people back into the hardest places with hope. You have stood with me, prayed with me, and served with me, and I do not take that lightly. I love this house.

To my political minister and mentor, "The Advocate," Ramon Jackson, the greatest political mind that has crossed the bridge of time, thank you for teaching me everything I know about politics. This book would not have happened without you.

And to President Donald J. Trump, thank you for enduring what most people could not endure, and for carrying responsibility in a moment when leadership comes with a price. Thank you for making room for faith in the public square and allowing pastors to pray without apology.

To every reader, my aim is not to stir anger. My aim is to stir discernment. If this book helps you think clearly, speak responsibly, and refuse hate, then it did what I wrote it to do.

PREFACE

Before We Argue, Let Us Think

Before I say anything political, let me say something pastoral.

Donald J. Trump is the President of the United States of America.

Not a pastor.
Not a prophet.
Not a pope.
A president.

And like every leader God has ever used, he is a sinner in need of grace.

What troubles me is not disagreement. Disagreement is healthy. What troubles me is hatred—how easily it rolls off our tongues, how casually it lives in our churches, how often it replaces prayer, discernment, and truth.

Somewhere along the way, politics became louder than the presence of God.

I pastor in Detroit. I lead in a city where nearly every elected official is a Democrat. I have prayed publicly for President Biden. I have prayed for leaders whose platforms I do not agree with. Not because I support their policies—but because Scripture commands it.

The Church is not called to like leaders.

The Church is called to think, pray, and intercede.

When hatred becomes normalized, when rage replaces reason, we are no longer dealing with politics. We are dealing with something spiritual. Scripture warns us that in the last days, people would be lovers of themselves, haters of what is good, quick to anger, and slow to listen. We are watching that unfold in real time.

This book is not written to make Donald Trump look good.

It is written to expose lies.

Lies create anger.
Anger produces violence.
And the anger of man does not produce the righteousness of God.

I am asking Christians to do something radical in our current moment: slow down, ask better questions, and stop surrendering your thinking to talking points.

You do not have to agree with me.

But you do owe God discernment.

Let us tear down the strongholds,

not with outrage,

but with truth.

INTRODUCTION

Why This Book Had to Be Written

There is something happening in America that should concern every Christian, regardless of party, background, or preference.

We are no longer arguing about policies.
We are no longer debating ideas.
We are no longer disagreeing with restraint.

We are **hating**.

And hatred has found a comfortable home not just in culture, but in the Church.

I am not writing this book because Donald Trump needs defending. He doesn't. He is not fragile. He is not unaware of criticism. He does not require a pastor to shield him from outrage.

I am writing this book because Christians are losing their ability to think clearly.

Somewhere between social media, cable news, and political identity, we surrendered discernment for slogans. We began reacting instead of reasoning. Repeating instead of examining. And when that happens, the loudest voices, not the wisest ones, win.

As a pastor, I see the fruit of this every day.

I see believers who can quote headlines but not Scripture.
I see Christians who know what they oppose but cannot explain why.
I see anger baptized as righteousness and outrage masquerading as conviction.

That should trouble us.

Scripture tells us to be quick to listen, slow to speak, and slow to anger. Yet we have reversed the order. We speak first. We react faster. We listen last—if at all.

And the result is confusion.

This book exists because confusion is not neutral. Confusion creates fear. Fear produces anger. And anger, when left unchecked, leads to division, violence, and destruction.

We have already seen the cost of that.

This Is Not a Political Manual

Let me be clear about what this book is *not*.

This is not a campaign guide.
This is not a party platform.
This is not an argument that Donald Trump is a savior, a saint, or a substitute for Christ.

He is none of those.

This is a book about **lies,** specifically the most repeated lies used to justify hatred. Lies that are spoken so often they feel true. Lies that are rarely interrogated. Lies that shape emotions long before facts are examined.

The Bible tells us the enemy is the father of lies. And lies are never told simply to misinform—they are told to move people. To stir anger. To harden hearts. To divide communities.

That is why this matters.

When Christians repeat lies, knowingly or unknowingly, we do the enemy's work for him.

Why These Ten Reasons Matter

The ten reasons in this book are not random. They are the accusations I hear most often — from church members, from leaders, from media voices, and from people who have never met Donald Trump but are certain they hate him.

They usually sound like this:

• He is for the billionaire class.
• He is a felon.
• He is a dictator.
• He is cutting resources to the poor.
• He doesn't have the character to be president.
• He is going to establish Project 2025.

- He is a sexist.
- He is a racist.
- He is a threat to democracy.
- He was wrong about the election being stolen, and January 6 proves it.

These aren't subtle accusations. They're spoken openly and often.

And because they are repeated often enough, they are treated as settled truth.

My goal is not to tell you what to think.

My goal is to help you **think honestly** about what you've been told.

Each chapter takes one of these claims and does three things: it names it clearly, examines it carefully, and places it under the light of Scripture, reason, and lived experience.

You may still disagree when you finish.

But you will no longer be able to say you didn't understand the argument.

A Word to the Church

The Church was never called to be politically convenient.

We were called to be truthful.

That means asking uncomfortable questions, even when the answers disrupt our assumptions. It means refusing to outsource our moral reasoning to pundits. It means remembering that political identity is not the same as spiritual maturity.

If you are a Christian reading this, I am asking you to pause before you dismiss, defend, or react.

Read slowly.
Think carefully.
Test everything.

The Bible does not promise comfort to the Church. It promises clarity, if we are willing to seek it.

How to Read This Book

This book is not meant to be skimmed in anger or consumed as ammunition.

It is meant to be **engaged**.

Read one chapter at a time.
Sit with the arguments.
Look up the Scriptures.

Ask yourself hard questions.

And most importantly — *pray.*

Not for a politician.

Not for an outcome.
But for wisdom.

Because wisdom, not outrage, is what this moment requires.

CHAPTER 1

Reason #10:

He Is for the Billionaire Class

"He's for the billionaire class."

That accusation is usually stated as fact, not argument. It's said with certainty, often with anger, and rarely with explanation. For many people, it has become the foundation for everything else they believe about Donald Trump.

But before we repeat it, before we allow it to shape our emotions or justify our hatred, we have to ask a basic question:

Define it.

What does it actually mean to say a president is "for the billionaire class"?

Does it mean he protects wealthy interests at the expense of the poor?

Does it mean he governs to enrich his friends?

Does it mean he uses public office for private gain?

Because if that is what people are claiming, then logic, not loyalty, demands we examine the evidence.

And when we do, this accusation begins to collapse almost immediately.

The Lie Sounds Plausible—Until You Think

Donald Trump is wealthy. That much is obvious. And in a culture that equates wealth with corruption, the conclusion is easy: *he must be governing for people like himself.*

But assumptions are not analysis.

If Donald Trump were truly governing for the billionaire class, he would have done what nearly every politician before him has done: leave wealthy friends in the private sector, quietly award them contracts, and allow them to profit without scrutiny.

That is how influence normally works.

Instead, he did something unprecedented.

He brought some of the wealthiest people in the country **into public service**, where they were required to divest, disclose, and give up private business dealings.

That alone contradicts the accusation.

You cannot claim a man is enriching his friends while simultaneously forcing them to surrender their ability to profit.

That is not how corruption works.

Public Service Is Not a Profit Center

When you work for the federal government, you do not get to operate like a private executive. You cannot quietly cut deals. You cannot hide income streams. You cannot leverage your position for personal gain without disclosure.

• **Howard Lutnick** entered public service at personal cost.
• **Steve Witkoff** subjected to public disclosure and scrutiny.
• **Linda McMahon** left private success for government accountability.

These are not people who entered government to get rich.
They were already rich.

They entered government to **lose money**, lose privacy, and lose control.

If Donald Trump were building an administration to benefit the billionaire class, the last thing he would do is place billionaires under the microscope of public accountability.

That is not favoritism.
That is restraint.

The Inconsistency No One Explains

What makes this accusation especially dishonest is how selectively it is applied.

When people accuse Trump of governing for wealthy interests, they ignore the fact that previous administrations allowed family members to profit openly while in proximity to power.

They ignore corporate board seats.

They ignore foreign business entanglements.

They ignore private-sector enrichment that continued uninterrupted.

And yet, the outrage is reserved for the one president who disrupted that pattern.

That inconsistency matters.

Because outrage without consistency is not conviction—it is bias.

Stripped, Not Subsidized

Here is the truth many people refuse to acknowledge:

Donald Trump did not become wealthy because of politics.

He entered politics already wealthy.

Most politicians do the opposite. They arrive in office with modest means and leave extraordinarily enriched.

Trump entered office, and then:

• lost business opportunities
• faced financial penalties
• endured legal attacks
• surrendered privacy
• and absorbed personal cost

That is not the behavior of a man using office to enrich himself.

It is the behavior of someone willing to be stripped.

And whether you consider that noble or foolish, it is not consistent with the claim that he is governing to benefit the billionaire class.

A Biblical Lens on Power and the Poor

Scripture does not condemn wealth.
It condemns **unjust gain**.

Jesus did not rebuke those who had resources. He rebuked those who used power without mercy.

In Matthew 25:40, Jesus says:

> *"Truly, I say to you, as you did it to one of the least of these my brothers, you did it to me." (ESV)*

I know President Trump personally. And when he came to my church, he did not come to be surrounded by donors or elites. He came intentionally to be among the poor, the overlooked, and the forgotten.

That is not a talking point.
That is lived experience.

The lie survives because it is repeated, not because it is true.

Why This Lie Persists

This accusation remains powerful because it is emotionally satisfying.
It allows people to simplify a complex political figure into
a moral villain.

But simplicity is not wisdom.

Christians are not called to repeat what sounds good.
We are called to test what is true.

And when we apply even basic scrutiny, the claim that Donald Trump
governs "for the billionaire class" does not withstand examination.

What Christians Must Do Instead

Before we condemn, we must define.
Before we repeat, we must reason.
Before we hate, we must think.

This chapter is not asking you to like Donald Trump.

It is asking you to stop repeating something you have not examined.

Because lies, especially comfortable ones, do more damage to the Church than they ever do to politicians.

The Political Shortcut That Feels Moral

Calling Donald Trump "for the billionaire class" is a shortcut. It allows people to bypass thinking while still feeling morally superior.

It sounds compassionate.
It sounds righteous.
It sounds like concern for the poor.

But sounding right and being right are not the same thing.

The Bible warns us about this tendency. Proverbs tells us that *"The simple believe everything, but the prudent give thought to their steps."* Wisdom requires examination. It requires slowing down long enough to ask whether a claim is actually true—or merely popular.

Most people never take that step.

Instead, they confuse outcomes with intentions. They see tax policy, business language, or corporate familiarity and assume motive. But assumptions are not discernment. And discernment is not optional for believers.

Wealth Is Not the Enemy. Injustice Is.

Scripture never teaches that wealth itself is sinful. What Scripture condemns is **unjust gain**, exploitation, and the abuse of power.

That distinction matters.

If wealth alone disqualified someone from leadership, then Scripture would contradict itself. Abraham was wealthy. Job was wealthy. David was wealthy. Joseph administered the wealth of an empire. What God judged was not what they possessed, but how they stewarded power.

So when people accuse Trump of governing for the billionaire class, the real question becomes this:

Where is the injustice?

Where is the policy that intentionally crushed the poor to enrich the wealthy?

Where is the evidence that public office was used to privately profit?

Where is the documented transfer of power from the vulnerable to the elite?

Those questions are almost never answered, because they are almost never asked.

The Myth of the "Rich Man's Presidency"

Here is something most critics overlook:

Donald Trump governed during a period when wages rose, employment increased, and opportunity expanded across racial and economic lines. Those gains were not limited to boardrooms. They were felt in communities like mine.

I pastor in Detroit. I don't speak from theory. I speak from proximity.

I watched people who had been locked out of opportunity step back into work. I watched businesses reopen. I watched confidence return to communities that had been written off for decades.

If a presidency truly existed only to benefit the wealthy, you would not see that kind of downstream impact.

You would see consolidation, not expansion.

Why the Church Should Be Especially Careful Here

Christians should be the first to resist lazy narratives, especially narratives that rely on envy, resentment, or moral posturing.

When we repeat accusations without examination, we don't just misjudge a leader. We train ourselves to think poorly. And poor thinking leads to poor witness.

The Church loses credibility when it speaks confidently about things it has not studied carefully.

We are not called to echo the loudest voices in culture.
We are called to test every spirit, every claim, every narrative.

That includes political ones.

The Real Reason This Accusation Persists

This lie survives because it offers emotional relief.

If Donald Trump is simply "for the billionaire class," then people don't have to wrestle with uncomfortable truths, like why political systems fail, why policies don't work as promised, or why dependency often replaces empowerment.

It shifts blame upward without requiring accountability inward.

But truth does not work that way.

Truth demands responsibility.
Truth demands honesty.
Truth demands courage.

A Final Word on This Accusation

You may still dislike Donald Trump after reading this chapter. That is not the issue.

The issue is whether you are willing to stop repeating something simply because it feels right.

As Christians, we are accountable not just for what we believe, but for **why** we believe it.

The claim that Donald Trump governed "for the billionaire class" does not survive honest scrutiny.

CHAPTER 2

Reason #9:

He Is a Felon

"He is a felon."

The word *felon* lands heavy.

People don't use it carefully. They use it like a gavel. Like a final sentence. Like it ends the conversation.

When people say it, they usually mean more than a conviction. They mean *disqualified*. They mean *unfit*. They mean *case closed*.

So let's slow this down and tell the truth without slogans.

Donald Trump **was convicted of felony counts in a New York court in 2024.** That is a matter of public record. Pretending otherwise does not serve truth, and it does not serve the Church.

But the way this word is now being used goes far beyond the facts.

He was convicted under a novel legal theory, elevated to felony status through a prosecutorial interpretation that is now under appeal.

He was not convicted of violence. He was not convicted of treason.

He was not convicted of selling state secrets. He was not convicted of harming the public in the way people *imply* when they say the word *felon* like it's a spiritual verdict.

And *that* distinction matters.

What the Record Actually Says

Here's what is plain and true:

- A jury convicted Trump on **34 counts of falsifying business records in the first degree** (a felony under New York law).
- In January 2025, the judge sentenced him to an **unconditional discharge**, meaning **no jail, no probation, no fine,** while the conviction still stands unless overturned.
- The case has continued through the appellate process, and Trump **formally appealed** the conviction in 2025.

So yes, the conviction exists. And yes, context exists, too.

The Church should be able to hold both without panic, spin, or selective memory.

When I Say "Novel Legal Theory," Here's What I Mean

Let me say this clearly: *the statute itself isn't new.*

New York law has long made falsifying business records a **misdemeanor** — *unless* prosecutors claim it was done with "intent to commit another crime or conceal the commission of another crime," which elevates it to a **felony.** That felony "upgrade" is written right into the law.

So what do people mean when they call this case "novel"?

They're usually talking about **how the felony element was argued and constructed**, the way the prosecution connected bookkeeping entries to "another crime," and the debates around what that "other crime" was and how clearly it was specified and proven.

Legal analysts noted early on that the indictment did not spell out the "other crime" on its face the way many people expect in ordinary cases, and that became one of the points of controversy and argument surrounding the case.

And that's the part that matters for the reader, because it explains why two people can say two different things at the same time:

• One person can say, "He was convicted."

• Another can say, "And the legal route to felony status is being challenged and appealed."

Both can be true at once, and the believer's job is not to scream one truth loud enough to bury the other.

Conviction Is Not the End of the Conversation

In American law, an appeal exists for a reason: to review whether law was applied correctly and whether procedure was handled justly.

Now, let's be honest: **a conviction is still a conviction while the appeal is pending.** That's why the label sticks in headlines. But Christians aren't called to live by headlines. We are called to live by truth.

Scripture warns us not to decide a matter before we've heard it fully. Scripture warns us about bearing false witness. Scripture tells us to be quick to listen and slow to speak.

That doesn't mean "deny reality." It means *don't weaponize it.*

Why This Label Is So Powerful

Calling someone a *felon* is a way to shut down thought.

Once the label sticks, the reasoning stops:

No questions. No standards. No consistency.
No examination of motive, precedent, or process.

And that should concern believers — not because we're protecting a man from accountability, but because we're watching a culture learn how to erase people with a single word.

When "felon" becomes a substitute for discernment, Christians don't just lose nuance, we lose moral seriousness.

Character, Fitness, and the Office of President

The Presidency is not a pastoral office.

It never has been.

The Constitution sets only a few basic qualifications for the President: age, natural-born citizenship, and residency — it does **not** include a "criminal record" clause.

So when people use *felon* to imply "therefore he cannot serve," they're often mixing legal categories with emotional categories, and then calling it righteousness.

The real question is not, "Has this man been convicted?"

The deeper question is: **What standard are we using, and are we applying it evenly?**

Because if conviction alone is the new moral bar for the public square, then it must be applied consistently across parties, across systems, and across history.

Most people don't want consistency. They want a label that ends the argument.

Why This Matters for the Church

The Church is not called to protect men from accountability.

But neither is the Church called to outsource judgment to outrage.

So yes, tell the truth: he was convicted.

And also tell the truth: the legal construction of this case, and the questions surrounding it, are part of what is being argued on appeal.

Truth requires more than a label.

Discernment requires more than repetition.

And the Gospel demands more than certainty without examination.

CHAPTER 3

Reason #8:

He Is a Dictator

"He is a dictator."

That word gets used quickly and carelessly. It is meant to end debate, not invite understanding. Once someone is labeled a dictator, everything they do is reinterpreted through fear. Authority becomes tyranny. Enforcement becomes oppression. Leadership becomes abuse.

But words matter.

And before Christians repeat this accusation, we have a responsibility to understand what we are actually saying.

Because calling a president a dictator is not a metaphor. It is a claim about power, structure, and control. And if it is true, it should be provable.

What a Dictator Actually Is

- A dictator is someone who governs without accountability.
- A dictator does not seek approval.
- A dictator does not submit to law.

• A dictator does not share power.
• A dictator does not tolerate opposition.

A dictator rules by force, not process.

That definition matters, because when we apply it honestly, the accusation begins to unravel.

Authority Is Not Tyranny

One of the great confusions of our time is the belief that any use of authority is automatically abusive.

That idea is not biblical.

Scripture teaches that authority, when rightly exercised, is a form of stewardship. Romans 13 tells us that governing authority exists to restrain evil and protect the innocent. Order is not oppression. Enforcement is not cruelty.

The problem is not authority.
The problem is **unchecked authority**.

And that is exactly why America was designed with three separate branches of government.

A Constitutional Reality Check

The United States is not governed by one man.

Power is divided between:
• the executive branch
• the legislative branch
• the judicial branch

A president cannot pass laws alone.
A president cannot fund government alone.
A president cannot rule by decree without challenge.

Even policies Donald Trump supported were debated, voted on, blocked, modified, and litigated.

That is not dictatorship.
That is governance within constraint.

Ironically, the very fact that his decisions were challenged in court is proof that he was not ruling as a dictator.

The National Guard Myth

One of the most common examples people use to justify this accusation is the use of the National Guard.

But here is a fact many people do not know:
More than two dozen American presidents have deployed the National Guard.

Republicans.
Democrats.
Progressives.
Conservatives.

Calling in the National Guard to protect citizens, restore order, or respond to crisis is not tyranny. It is literally part of the president's job.

In communities like mine—urban communities plagued by violence—people are not afraid of protection. They are begging for it.

There is not a single Black mother in America who wants her child dodging bullets in the name of political ideology.

Safety is not oppression.
Order is not injustice.

Judges, Power, and the Irony of the Accusation

Here is where the accusation becomes especially ironic.

Those most insulated from accountability in our system are not presidents. They are judges.

Federal judges are appointed for life. They are not voted out. They do not face the electorate. Their power is permanent.

If anyone comes close to unchecked authority, it is not the executive branch, it is the judiciary.

Yet the word *dictator* is almost never applied there.

Why?

Because the accusation is not about structure.
It is about disagreement.

Scripture and Liberty

The Bible tells us plainly: *"Where the Spirit of the Lord is, there is liberty."* (2 Corinthians 3:17)

Liberty does not mean the absence of rules.
It means the presence of righteous order.

America's founders understood this. That is why they built a system that distributes power, limits authority, and allows for correction.

Donald Trump did not dismantle that system.
He operated within it—often contentiously, sometimes imperfectly—but always within its boundaries.

A dictator would not tolerate resistance.
A dictator would not submit to process.
A dictator would not wait for approval.

And yet, approval was sought, denied, negotiated, and revisited repeatedly.

Why This Accusation Persists

Calling Donald Trump a dictator relieves people of responsibility.

If he is a tyrant, then resistance becomes virtue and rage becomes justified. Nuance disappears. Thinking stops.

But truth is rarely that convenient.

This accusation survives because it is emotionally effective, not because it is structurally accurate.

What Christians Must Remember

Christians are not called to react to fear.
We are called to discern truth.

We are not called to confuse enforcement with evil.
We are called to judge righteously.

Words like *dictator* should never be used casually, especially by people who claim to follow the One who warned us about bearing false witness.

A Final Word on This Claim

You may disagree with Donald Trump's policies.
You may dislike his style.
You may oppose his decisions.

But calling him a dictator without evidence is not wisdom—it is exaggeration.

And exaggeration, no matter how loudly repeated, does not become truth.

CHAPTER 4

Reason #7:

He Is Cutting Resources to the Poor

"He is cutting resources to the poor."

This accusation is usually delivered with moral certainty. It doesn't just criticize policy, it questions compassion. And for Christians, that makes it especially potent. No one wants to be associated with indifference toward suffering.

But before we accept this claim, we have to do something many people skip:

We have to understand how resources actually flow.

Because outrage without understanding is not compassion. It is manipulation.

The Confusion Between Government and Charity

One of the most common misunderstandings in this debate is the belief that the President of the United States can simply reach into a bank account and remove funding from food banks, shelters, or safety-net organizations.

That is not how it works.

Most compassion organizations, food pantries, shelters, community programs, are **private nonprofits**. They are funded through:

• private donations
• corporate sponsorships
• grants
• local and state budgets

Federal funding, when it exists at all, usually represents **a small percentage** of their overall operating budget.

A president does not control these organizations.
A president does not manage their accounts.
A president does not approve or deny their day-to-day funding.

So when people say, "He's cutting resources to the poor," the first question must be:

Which resources, exactly?

Budgets Are Set Before a President Takes Office

Here is another fact rarely mentioned.

Most government budgets are approved **before** a president ever takes office. Funding allocations are voted on by legislatures, approved by boards, and locked into place months—or years—in advance.

When President Trump took office, many of the budgets impacting social services were already passed under previous administrations.

To blame him for cuts that were never his to make is not just inaccurate, it's dishonest.

And dishonesty dressed up as compassion is still dishonesty.

The Detroit Reality Check

I pastor in Detroit. I don't speak about poverty from a distance.

I work alongside organizations that serve the poor every single day. I understand how funding works because I've had to understand it.

When resources increase or decrease in cities like mine, it is almost always the result of:

• local government decisions
• state allocations
• private donor behavior
• mismanagement or redirection of funds

Not presidential whim.

If a mayor reallocates millions of dollars locally,
the president didn't do that.

If a nonprofit closes because donations dried up,
the president didn't do that.

If leadership fails to steward resources wisely,
the president didn't do that.

Blaming Washington for every local failure is convenient,
but it is not truthful.

Compassion Is Not Centralized Control

Here is a hard truth the Church must grapple with:

When compassion becomes fully dependent on government,
it stops being compassion and becomes bureaucracy.

Biblical care for the poor has always flowed through **people, families,
communities,** and **the Church**—not distant federal agencies.

Jesus did not say, "When the government fed the hungry, you fed me."
He said, *"When you did it."*

That distinction matters.

Policies that empower local solutions, private charity, and community
engagement do not harm the poor. They often help them
more effectively.

Centralization feels compassionate.
But effectiveness is what actually lifts people out of poverty.

The Lie That Creates Anger

This accusation persists because it creates a sense of moral emergency.

If people believe a president is actively harming the poor, anger feels justified. Resistance feels righteous. Rage feels necessary.

But when that belief is built on misunderstanding—or worse, misinformation—it produces something dangerous.

The Bible warns us plainly:
The anger of man does not produce the righteousness of God.

Anger may feel productive.
But it rarely produces wisdom.

When Compassion Becomes a Political Weapon

Some organizations exist not to alleviate poverty, but to **manage it** and then use it as leverage.

That is uncomfortable to say, but it is true.

Entire systems have been built that profit from perpetual dependency. And when those systems are challenged, when accountability is demanded, critics cry cruelty.

But asking whether programs actually work is not hatred.
It is stewardship.

Christians should care not just about *intentions*, but about outcomes.

What Christians Must Remember

Christians are called to care for the poor.

But we are not called to suspend our thinking in the name
of compassion.

We are not called to believe every claim that sounds caring.
We are called to discern truth, steward resources, and pursue solutions
that actually restore dignity.

Compassion without clarity can do harm.

A Final Word on This Claim

You may disagree with how Donald Trump approaches poverty.
You may prefer different policies.
You may support broader federal involvement.

But the claim that he is personally cutting resources to the poor
does not survive honest examination.

And repeating it without understanding how systems actually work
does not honor the people it claims to protect.

CHAPTER 5

Reason #6:

He Doesn't Have the Character to be President

"He doesn't have the character to be president."

This accusation is usually framed as a moral verdict. It assumes the conclusion before the examination. And for many Christians, it feels decisive because character matters.

It should.

But before we repeat this claim, we need to ask a harder question:

What kind of character are we actually talking about?

Because the character required to pastor a church is not the same as the character required to lead a nation. And confusing the two has caused the Church to misjudge leadership for generations.

Pastor Standards vs. Presidential Responsibility

Scripture gives clear qualifications for pastors. They are high. They are demanding. They are spiritual. They are relational.

But Scripture does not give the same qualifications for kings, generals, or civil rulers.

Why?

Because those roles require a different kind of character.

A president is not called to shepherd souls.
A president is called to make decisions under pressure.
A president is called to confront enemies.
A president is called to endure conflict.
A president is called to act when consensus is impossible.

When Christians demand pastoral virtue from political office, they are asking leaders to be something God never required them to be.

The Biblical Pattern We Ignore

Throughout Scripture, God consistently used leaders who were flawed, broken, and often morally compromised, yet uniquely suited for the moment they were placed in.

- **Moses** was disqualified by temperament long before he was qualified by calling.

- **David's** moral failures were public and devastating.

- **Samson's** personal life was chaotic.

- **Cyrus** was a pagan king and still called God's instrument.

God never pretended these men were righteous in every way. He used them because they were **fit for the assignment**.

That pattern did not end in the Old Testament.

The Character Required to Withstand Pressure

Here is something many people underestimate:

It takes a particular kind of character to endure unrelenting opposition.

Donald Trump endured:

• multiple impeachments
• nonstop media hostility
• legal assaults
• financial attacks
• public humiliation
• assassination attempts

And he did not retreat.

You don't have to admire him to acknowledge that.

That kind of endurance is not accidental. It is a form of character—one that Scripture often calls perseverance.

And perseverance matters when a leader is carrying national responsibility.

Moral Failure vs. Functional Fitness

Some critics point to Trump's personal failures and say, "That disqualifies him."

But disqualifies him from what, exactly?

From preaching the gospel? Yes.
From shepherding a congregation? Absolutely.
From serving as a spiritual example? Possibly.

But the office of the presidency is not a pulpit.

The test is not moral flawlessness.
The test is whether someone can **carry authority without collapsing**.

History shows us that many leaders with pristine public personas failed under pressure, while deeply flawed men held the line.

Why This Accusation Resonates

This accusation persists because it allows Christians to feel morally clean while avoiding complexity.

It replaces discernment with distance.
It allows judgment without examination.
It simplifies leadership into virtue signaling.

But leadership, especially at the national level, is not simple.

And Scripture never promised us leaders who made us comfortable. It promised us leaders God could use.

A Word About Redemption

Christians should be the last people to believe someone is beyond redemption and the first to acknowledge that God can work through broken people.

Redemption does not erase consequences.
It does not rewrite the past.
But it does mean God is not finished with a person.

If Christians believe in grace only when it is theoretical—but reject it when it becomes politically inconvenient—we have misunderstood the gospel we claim to preach.

What Christians Must Decide

We have to decide whether we are evaluating presidents as:

• spiritual leaders
   or
• civil authorities

Because when we confuse those roles, we set standards no human being can meet, and then congratulate ourselves for rejecting them.

Character matters.
But so does calling.
So does assignment.
So does endurance.

A Final Word on This Claim

You may find Donald Trump's personal life troubling.
You may disagree with his tone.
You may wish he communicated differently.

But the claim that he lacks the character to be president misunderstands what the presidency requires.

And misunderstanding the assignment will always lead to misjudging the man.

CHAPTER 6

Reason #5:

He Is Going To Establish Project 2025

"He is going to establish Project 2025."

This accusation is often delivered with alarm. It is framed as a warning, not a claim, something dark, coordinated, and inevitable. For many people, the mere mention of *Project 2025* is enough to trigger fear.

But fear is a poor substitute for understanding.

Before Christians repeat this accusation, we need to slow down and ask a basic question:

What is Project 2025—and what is it not?

What Project 2025 Actually Is

Project 2025 is not a law.
It is not an executive order.
It is not a secret government plan.

It is a policy proposal authored by the Heritage Foundation, a conservative think tank that has been publishing policy recommendations for decades.

That distinction matters.

Think tanks do not govern.
They advise.
They recommend.
They propose.

Every major political ideology in America has them.

Progressive think tanks write policy roadmaps.
Liberal coalitions publish governing agendas.
Advocacy groups release platforms every election cycle.

Project 2025 is one of many such documents.

Treating it as if it is a binding mandate misunderstands how American government works.

A Think Tank Is Not a Throne

The Heritage Foundation does not elect presidents.
It does not pass legislation.
It does not enforce policy.

It publishes ideas.

And ideas, no matter how strongly worded, do not become law without:

- congressional approval
- executive action
- judicial review

Fear thrives when people collapse these distinctions.

But Christians should not fear ideas.
We should examine them.

The Myth of a Secret Plan

One reason this accusation resonates is because it sounds conspiratorial.

"They're planning something."
"They've already decided."
"Democracy is about to end."

But secrecy is not what is happening here.

Project 2025 is public.
Its authors are known.
Its arguments are accessible.

You can read it.
You can disagree with it.
You can critique it.

That transparency alone undermines the narrative of a hidden authoritarian takeover.

Authoritarianism does not announce itself in white papers.

Presidents Govern Through Process

Even if a president agrees with portions of a think tank's recommendations, nothing happens automatically.

Presidents:

• negotiate
• compromise
• adjust
• abandon proposals
• face resistance
• encounter legal limits

No president, Republican or Democrat, has ever governed by adopting a think tank's agenda wholesale.

The idea that Donald Trump would or could simply "establish Project 2025" ignores political reality.

America does not work that way.

Why This Accusation Persists

This accusation survives because it is emotionally effective.

It allows critics to frame disagreement as danger.
It turns policy debate into moral panic.
It replaces analysis with alarm.

And once fear takes hold, nuance disappears.

But Scripture repeatedly warns us against fear-based reasoning.

Fear clouds judgment.
Fear accelerates anger.
Fear weakens discernment.

Christians are not called to fear proposals.
We are called to test them.

Disagreement Is Not Destruction

You may disagree with elements of Project 2025.
You may oppose its priorities.
You may reject its assumptions.

That is fair.

But disagreement does not equal doom.

A healthy democracy debates ideas.
It does not collapse because they exist.

Calling every conservative policy proposal a threat to our constitutional order empties the phrase of meaning.

What Christians Must Remember

Christians should be the calmest people in the room,
not the most alarmed.

We are called to:

• understand before reacting
• evaluate before condemning
• reason before repeating

When fear becomes the loudest voice, truth rarely follows.

A Final Word on This Claim

You may believe Project 2025 contains ideas you find troubling.
You may hope none of its recommendations are adopted.
You may advocate strongly against it.

But the claim that Donald Trump is going to "establish Project 2025" as some sweeping, uncontested program does not survive honest scrutiny.

Ideas are proposed.

Power is contested.

Process matters.

And fear, no matter how loudly repeated, does not become truth.

CHAPTER 7

Reason #4:

He Is a Sexist

"He is a sexist."

That accusation gets said like it's settled. Like there's nothing left to discuss. Once that label gets attached to a man, people stop listening. Every decision becomes evidence. Every sentence becomes proof.

But if we're going to accuse a man of something that serious, we at least owe the truth the courtesy of a definition.

Because disagreement is not discrimination.
Tone is not tyranny.
And offense is not proof.

So let's start here:

What does sexism actually mean?

What Sexism Actually Is

Sexism is not saying something unpopular.
Sexism is not speaking bluntly.

Sexism is not refusing to adopt someone else's ideological language.

Sexism is the **denial of opportunity or authority because of sex**.

That's the standard.

So if a man is sexist, you should be able to show:

• women being blocked,
• women being denied authority,
• women being refused leadership,
• women being shut out of decision-making.

That's what sexism looks like.

Now let's look at the record.

Look at the Actual Record

People keep saying he hates women. But when you look at the facts, the narrative falls apart.

President Trump was the first president to appoint a **female Chief of Staff**. That's not symbolic. That position is one of the most powerful roles in the White House. The Chief of Staff controls access, operations, strategy, and execution. You don't put someone there unless you trust their leadership.

And it didn't stop there.

Look at Susie Wiles.
She wasn't standing in the background. She was running strategy. She was shaping outcomes. She was trusted with real responsibility, not ceremonial influence.

Look at Brooke Rollins.
Policy. Governance. Decision-making. She wasn't there to smile for the cameras. She was there to help govern a nation.

Look at Pam Bondi.
Attorney General. Law enforcement. Legal authority. You don't put a woman in charge of enforcing the law if you believe she is incapable.

Look at Laura Chavez.
Public leadership. Administration. Influence. Real work.

And then look at **Alice Marie Johnson**.

That one alone dismantles the narrative.

She wasn't used. She wasn't paraded. She wasn't tokenized. She was heard. Her voice mattered. Her advocacy mattered. Her life mattered. And she was given authority—not pity.

So when people say, "He hates women," I ask a simple question:

Show me the doors he closed.

Because what I see are doors being opened.

Sexism doesn't look like this.

Tone Is Not Tyranny

A lot of this accusation has nothing to do with opportunity
and everything to do with emotion.

People don't like how he talks.
They don't like how direct he is.
They don't like how unfiltered he is.

Fine.

But not liking a man's personality is not proof that he hates women.

Some people don't want leadership. They want affirmation.
They want safety language.
They want a performance that makes them feel comfortable.

But presidents aren't elected to manage feelings.
They're elected to govern.

And governing requires firmness.

Firm doesn't mean sexist.

Policy Disagreement Is Not Hatred

Sometimes this accusation is really about policy.

Disagree on certain issues (family, gender, culture), and suddenly it becomes, "You hate women."

No. That means you disagree.

Christians, of all people, should understand the difference between disagreement and discrimination.

You can debate policy.
You can argue philosophy.
You can reject modern ideological frameworks.

But to call a man sexist, you have to prove what sexism actually is:

denying opportunity because of sex.

That proof isn't there.

What Christians Must Remember

The Bible honors women.
The Bible elevates women.
The Bible protects women.

And the Bible also refuses to lie.

Christians are not allowed to accuse casually.
We don't get to label people because it feels righteous.
Justice requires honesty.
And honesty requires definitions.

A Final Word on This Claim

You may not like Donald Trump's tone.
You may not like his style.
You may wish he communicated differently.

But the accusation that he is a sexist does not survive honest scrutiny.

Because sexism closes doors.

And the record shows women leading, deciding, governing,
and influencing at the highest levels.

That is not how sexism functions.

CHAPTER 8

Reason #3:

He Is a Racist

"He is a racist."

That accusation gets said quickly. Loudly. Often without explanation. And once it's said, many people feel there's nothing left to discuss.

But racism is not a vibe.
It is not a feeling.
And it is not a slogan.

If we're going to accuse a man of racism, we need to be clear about what racism actually is.

Because words this serious deserve definitions.

What Racism Actually Is

Racism is not disliking someone.
Racism is not disagreeing with someone.
Racism is not cultural discomfort or personal preference.

Racism is **closing the door of opportunity to someone because of the color of their skin.**

That's it.

Racism functions in very specific ways:

- **Passing over the most qualified person** because of skin color.
- **Denying opportunity** through law or practice.
- **Shutting doors deliberately**, not accidentally.

Preference is human.

How Racism Operates

Racism operates by:

- **Denying access** to opportunity.
- **Withholding authority** from qualified people.
- **Blocking advancement** through exclusion.

And when we define it that way, the accusation becomes testable.

If racism is real, it should show up consistently.
It shouldn't appear on cue.

The Accusation Didn't Exist Until It Did

Here's something people don't like to talk about.

Donald Trump wasn't widely labeled a racist for decades. He was known long before politics. But once he stepped into the presidential race—and especially once he became president—that accusation got louder, not because his whole life changed overnight, but because the moment changed.

That should at least cause us to pause.

Look at the Doors That Were Opened

I'm not talking theory. I'm talking lived reality.

If Donald Trump were a racist, I wouldn't have been invited to stand on the **largest political stage in the world** and pray.

You don't platform someone you despise.
You don't elevate someone you want to silence.
You don't give access to someone you believe is inferior.

And it didn't stop there.

I was welcomed into the White House.
I was seated at tables of influence.
I was heard, not tolerated.

Racism doesn't look like that.

Racism Is About Access, Not Affection

Here's where people get confused.

Racism is not:

• **Disliking someone personally.**
• **Lacking emotional warmth.**
• **Rejecting cultural sameness.**

Racism functions in very specific ways:

• **The most qualified person passed over** because of skin color.
• **Opportunity denied** by law or by practice.
• **Doors shut deliberately**, not accidentally.

Preference is human.
Prejudice is sin.
Racism, as it functions in systems, is about **denial of opportunity**.

A Personal Reality

And let me say this plainly.

I'm married to a woman of a different race.

That doesn't make me immune from sin, and it doesn't give me moral credit. But it does mean I live every day in an interracial family.

So when people casually throw the word racist around, I don't hear it as theory. I hear it as something that touches my home, my marriage, and my children.

Racism isn't about who you love.
It's about who you lock out.

And those are not the same thing.

What I've Seen in My Own Community

Let me make this practical — not political.

I pastor in a Black community. I don't talk about economics from a distance. I walk these streets. I know these families. I've watched neighborhoods change in real time.

There was a time when Black-owned businesses lined certain corridors in my area. Barbershops. Restaurants. Corner stores. Places where Black families worked, built, and passed something down.

Then illegal immigration exploded, not legal immigration, not people doing it the *right* way — **illegal immigration.**

And what happened?

Black businesses disappeared.

Not because Black people stopped working.
Not because we stopped building.
But because underground economies don't play by the same rules.

When people operate outside the law:

- **They don't pay the same taxes.**
- **They don't follow the same regulations.**
- **They don't carry the same costs.**

And when that happens, lawful businesses, often Black-owned businesses, get pushed out.

That's not a theory, that's lived experience.

And saying that out loud does not make someone racist.

It makes them honest.

Racism Is Not Telling the Truth About Systems

Here's the lie we've been told:

That if you point out how illegal systems harm Black communities, you must hate immigrants.

That's false.

You can support legal immigration **and** oppose illegal systems that crush lawful opportunity. You can also care about people and **care** about order.

In fact, you have to, if you care about justice.

Because when systems reward lawlessness, the people who suffer first are usually the poor, and disproportionately, Black Americans.

Ignoring that reality doesn't make you compassionate.
It makes you silent.

Racism Is Inefficient

Here's another truth people avoid.

Racism is expensive.

If you're running a business, a city, or a nation, you cannot afford to reject the best people simply because of race. You lose talent. You lose innovation. You lose effectiveness.

No serious leader does that.

If you want results, you open doors to the most capable people, regardless of skin color.

That's not ideology.
That's reality.

Why This Accusation Persists

This accusation remains powerful because it shuts down conversation.

Once someone is labeled racist:

- **Their arguments no longer matter.**
- **Their policies stop being examined.**
- **Their outcomes are never evaluated.**

The label becomes a shortcut.

But shortcuts are not truth.

Christians are not allowed to skip examination just because a word carries emotional weight.

What Christians Must Remember

Scripture is clear: God shows no partiality.

And neither should we.

That means we don't excuse real racism.
But it also means we don't invent it.

Bearing false witness is still a sin — even when it feels justified.

A Final Word on This Claim

You may dislike Donald Trump.
You may disagree with his policies.
You may oppose his leadership style.

But the claim that he is a racist does not survive honest scrutiny when racism is defined correctly.

Because racism closes doors.

And the record shows doors being opened publicly, visibly, and repeatedly, while illegal systems that harm Black opportunity are finally being named.

That is not racism.

That is reality.

CHAPTER 9

Reason #2:

He Is a "Threat to Democracy." *Or So They Say.*

"He is a threat to democracy."

That phrase gets repeated so often it starts to sound self-evident. It's said with urgency, with fear, and sometimes with moral certainty. For many people, it feels like the final word.

But before Christians repeat it, we need to slow down and ask a question almost no one asks:

What do people actually mean when they say "democracy"?

Because words matter. And when words are used loosely, they don't produce clarity. They produce fear.

What People Usually Mean

When most people say democracy, they are usually talking about a few basic ideas:

- The right to vote
- The ability to choose leaders
- Freedom to disagree
- The belief that power belongs to the people

Those instincts aren't wrong. But they are incomplete.

America was never designed as a pure democracy, where majority rule overrides all restraint. America was designed as a **constitutional republic**, with democratic processes governed by law.

That distinction is not technical.
It is foundational.

Why the Distinction Matters

A pure democracy concentrates power in the moment.
A constitutional republic restrains power over time.

In a democracy, fifty-one percent can rule the other forty-nine.
In a constitutional republic, even the majority is limited by law.

That is why America has:

- **A written Constitution**
- **Separation of powers**
- **Checks and balances**
- **Independent courts**
- **A legislature that restrains the executive**

These systems exist for one reason:
to prevent any single person, or any single majority,
from becoming absolute.

So when someone says, "He is a threat to democracy,"
the real question becomes:

A threat to what, exactly?

Disagreement Is Not Destruction

Much of what gets labeled a "threat to democracy" is simply
disagreement with policy.

Immigration enforcement.
Judicial appointments.
Election procedures.
Executive authority.

Disagreeing with how power is exercised is not the same as dismantling
the system itself.

In fact, disagreement is one of the signs that a constitutional republic
is functioning.

A system that collapses because people argue about policy
is not fragile—it's fake.

What a Real Threat Would Look Like

If a president were truly a threat to the constitutional order, you would see certain things happen:

- **Courts would be silenced,** not empowered.
- **Judges would be ignored,** not obeyed.
- **Elections would be canceled,** not contested through legal channels.
- **Opposition would be outlawed,** not amplified.

That is not what happened.

What Actually Happened

During President Trump's first administration:

- **Courts blocked** his policies.
- **Judges ruled against** his decisions.
- **States resisted** federal action.
- **Congress withheld** approvals.

That is not authoritarian collapse.

That is **institutional resistance functioning as designed.**

A president who is constantly challenged, restrained, and checked is not operating with unchecked power.

He is operating inside a system that still works.

The Irony No One Talks About

Here is the irony most people miss.

While Donald Trump is accused of being a "threat to democracy," unelected judges are often celebrated for overriding the decisions of elected officials.

When judges begin to substitute their will for lawfully enacted policy, that is not democracy or republican governance at all.

That is judicial overreach.

And Christians should care about that.

Because authority that is unaccountable is far more dangerous than authority that is elected and restrained.

Fear Thrives on Imprecise Language

The phrase "threat to democracy" is powerful because it is vague.

It doesn't require definition.
It doesn't require evidence.
It doesn't require explanation.

It simply creates alarm.

But Christians are not called to operate in alarm.
We are called to operate in truth.

And truth requires precision.

What Christians Should Ask Instead

Instead of repeating slogans, Christians should ask better questions:

• **What constitutional authority is being violated?**
• **What legal process has been ignored?**
• **What law has been suspended?**
• **What check or balance has failed?**

If those questions can't be answered, the accusation is not an argument.

It's a feeling.

And feelings, no matter how intense, are not evidence.

Order Is Not Oppression

Biblical faith is not allergic to authority.

Scripture teaches order.
It teaches restraint.
It teaches accountability.

A constitutional republic reflects those values far more faithfully than emotional slogans ever will.

Calling order "tyranny" doesn't make it so.
Calling enforcement "oppression" doesn't make it unjust.

Sometimes what people fear is not dictatorship, but discipline.

A Final Word on This Claim

You may disagree with Donald Trump's policies.
You may dislike his style.
You may oppose his decisions.

But the claim that he is a "threat to democracy" collapses once language is clarified and systems are examined honestly.

Because a man constantly restrained by courts, checked by Congress, resisted by states, and challenged by the media is not dismantling the system.

He is operating inside it.

And that matters.

CHAPTER 10

Reason #1:

January 6:
The Lie That Sealed the Verdict

There is no accusation more powerful, more emotionally charged, or more frequently repeated than this one.

January 6.

For many Americans, those two words end the conversation. They are treated as proof, verdict, and motive all at once. Once invoked, no further examination is expected. The case is considered closed.

That is why this accusation matters more than any other.

Because it didn't merely challenge a presidency — it **sealed a verdict without a trial.**

Why January 6 Became the Final Judgment

January 6 did not become decisive because it was fully understood. It became decisive because it was emotionally overwhelming.

Images looped.
Language escalated.
Fear hardened into certainty.

In moments like that, people reach for resolution before they reach for truth.

That impulse is human.
But it is not how justice works.

When Emotion Replaces Examination

What happened on January 6 was real.
People were present.
Buildings were breached.
Disorder occurred.

But acknowledging chaos is not the same as assigning guilt accurately.

Emotion can tell us something went wrong.
It cannot tell us **who is responsible, in what way, and to what extent.**

Those conclusions take time.
They require evidence.
They require restraint.

When emotion outruns examination, verdicts get reached before facts are weighed.

Why Christians Must Pause Here

Scripture is clear about moments like this.

We are warned to:

• **Hear a matter fully** before judging it.
• **Refuse false witness,** even when it feels justified.
• **Test claims carefully,** not absorb them because they are popular or repeated.

Yet January 6 became a moment where asking questions itself was treated as guilt.

That should give believers pause.
Because certainty without truth is not righteousness.

It's convenience.

Questioning Is Not Incitement

One of the most important distinctions lost in this conversation is simple but critical:

Questioning an outcome is not the same as inciting violence.

Throughout American history, elections have been contested.
Legal challenges have been filed.
Recounts have been demanded.
Outcomes have been disputed.

That process, when pursued through lawful channels, is not rebellion. It is part of the system.

The question is not whether people protested.
The question is whether lawful inquiry was replaced
by unlawful instruction.

Those two things are not the same — even though they were treated as if they were.

What This Chapter Will and Will Not Do

This chapter will not excuse violence.
It will not justify disorder.
It will not minimize wrongdoing where it occurred.

But it will also not accept conclusions that were reached emotionally, politically, or prematurely.

This chapter will examine:

• what was claimed
• what was proven
• what was assumed
• and what was never examined at all

Because truth deserves more than repetition.

Why This Matters Beyond One Man

This is not only about Donald Trump.

It's about precedent.

If an accusation can be locked in place without full examination,
and if questions themselves can be treated as crimes,
then truth becomes secondary to consensus.

And when consensus replaces truth, justice becomes selective.

Christians should be concerned about that.

The Posture Required Going Forward

This isn't a moment for outrage.
It isn't a moment for denial.
And it certainly isn't a moment for blind loyalty.

What's required here is sober discernment.

The kind that listens carefully.
The kind that distinguishes accusation from proof.
The kind that refuses to rush judgment just to feel settled.

That posture isn't weakness.

It's wisdom.

When Asking Questions Became the Crime

Before January 6 became a verdict, there was something else that happened quietly and much earlier.

Questions were raised.

Not riots.
Not violence.
Questions.

About process.
About access.
About irregularities.
About procedures that didn't look the same everywhere.

For generations, asking questions like these was normal. It was legal. It was expected. In some cases, it was even celebrated.

But in this moment, questioning itself was rebranded.

From Inquiry to Insurrection

What changed wasn't the act of questioning.
What changed was how questioning was described.

Legal challenges were reframed as rebellion.
Requests for audits were framed as sabotage.
Affidavits were dismissed before they were read.

The message became clear very quickly:

You are allowed to vote.
You are not allowed to ask what happened afterward.

That should concern anyone who believes in ordered liberty.

Affidavits Are Not Conspiracies

An affidavit is not a rumor.
It is not social media speculation.
It is sworn testimony, given under penalty of perjury.

That matters.

Affidavits don't decide outcomes by themselves, but they do demand examination. They require review. They deserve to be tested, not mocked.

Yet many affidavits were never meaningfully examined at all.

They were dismissed because acknowledging them would require slowing down.

And slowing down was inconvenient.

Why Slowing Down Matters

Justice is rarely fast.
Truth is rarely tidy.

When outcomes are rushed, mistakes get buried.
When narratives harden too quickly, inquiry becomes suspect.

Scripture warns against this kind of haste.

We are warned to:

• hear a matter fully before judging it
• refuse false witness, even when it feels justified
• test claims carefully, not absorb them because they are popular
  or repeated

That wisdom doesn't disappear in election years.

The Pressure to Agree

As questions surfaced, another force appeared: pressure.

Pressure to comply.
Pressure to stay quiet.
Pressure to affirm conclusions before processes were complete.

For many leaders, silence felt safer than scrutiny.

And for many citizens, agreement felt easier than investigation.

But agreement under pressure is not consensus.

It's conformity.

What Was Lost in the Rush

In the race to settle the story, something important was lost.

Distinction.

The difference between:

• questioning and inciting
• protesting and rioting
• legal challenge and unlawful action

When those distinctions disappear, responsibility becomes blurry.

And when responsibility becomes blurry, justice becomes careless.

Why This Still Matters

This conversation didn't end on January 6.

The precedent remains.

If asking questions can be criminalized after the fact, then inquiry itself becomes dangerous. And when inquiry becomes dangerous, truth becomes fragile.

That isn't a political concern.

It's a moral one.

When Testimony Was Ignored

At some point, this stopped being abstract.

Names were attached.
Statements were signed.
Affidavits were submitted.

These were not anonymous posts or viral clips. These were individuals willing to put their names, reputations, and legal standing on the line.

People like **Jacqueline Theresa Williams.**
Fode Gibson.
Melissa Love.
Gerald Johnson.
Kenneth Goldsmith.

These were not political celebrities.
They were ordinary citizens.

And in several cases, they were people who had little to gain and much to lose.

Why These Names Matter

These individuals did not claim to control outcomes.
They did not claim to know motives.
They testified to what they personally experienced.

Some stated they never registered to vote, yet records showed ballots associated with their names.

Others testified to irregular access, handling, or registration procedures that raised legitimate questions.

That kind of testimony does not automatically prove fraud.

But it does demand examination.

In any other context, whether employment law, civil court, or criminal proceedings, sworn testimony is not brushed aside because it is inconvenient.

It is reviewed.

The Cost of Speaking Up

It's easy to talk about courage in theory.

It's harder to recognize it in ordinary people.

Submitting an affidavit carries risk.
Perjury is a serious charge.

False statements carry real consequences.

These were not affluent insiders protected by influence.

Many were working-class citizens. Some were from communities that do not typically benefit from political power.

For them, speaking up was not performative.

It was costly.

Why Dismissing Them Was Easier

Engaging these testimonies would have required time.
It would have required investigation.
It would have required patience.

Instead, dismissal was faster.

Labels replaced listening.
Mockery replaced inquiry.
Certainty replaced process.

That shift didn't happen because the system was strong.

It happened because the system was tired.

The Pattern That Emerged

What made this moment different was not the existence of questions — America has seen those before.

It was the response.

Instead of:

• review
• examination
• clarification

There was:

• ridicule
• silencing
• accusation

The very act of questioning was reframed as an attack.

That is a dangerous precedent.

Why Christians Should Care About Process

Christians understand something foundational:

Truth is not afraid of scrutiny.

Scripture repeatedly affirms process:

- witnesses matter
- testimony matters
- examination matters

Justice does not fear the light.
It welcomes it.

When testimony is dismissed without review,
the issue is no longer political.

It's moral.

What Was Never Claimed

It's important to be clear about what these individuals did not claim.

They did not claim omniscience.
They did not claim conspiracy.
They did not claim certainty about outcomes.

They claimed experience.

And experience, when sworn under oath, deserves examination —
even if it complicates the story.

Why This Was the Flash Point

Once sworn testimony was treated as treason,
the conversation shifted permanently.

Inquiry was no longer allowed.
Distinction was no longer made.
Process was no longer trusted.

At that point, January 6 stopped being about events.

It became a tool.

A way to end debate.
A way to close inquiry.
A way to seal the verdict.

What Was Proven and What Was Not

It is important to be honest about limits.

Not every question raised after the election was proven true.
Not every claim held up under scrutiny.
Not every concern pointed to the same conclusion.

But that was never the standard.

The standard was whether questions were allowed to be asked and
whether sworn testimony was allowed to be examined without being
treated as treason.

On that point, the record is clear.

When Process Became Suspicion

Once inquiry itself was labeled dangerous, the rules changed.

Questioning was no longer framed as civic engagement.
It was framed as moral failure.

To ask was to signal disloyalty.
To investigate was to invite accusation.
To slow down was to be blamed for what came next.

That shift did not protect truth.

It protected a narrative.

Why January 6 Became the Final Answer

January 6 did not become central because it explained everything.

It became central because it ended everything.

Once invoked, it allowed no further distinction:

• between peaceful protest and criminal action
• between legal challenge and unlawful behavior
• between responsibility and proximity

Everything collapsed into a single story.

And once that story hardened, it no longer mattered what questions came before or what testimony followed after.

The verdict had already been sealed.

The Moral Cost of a Sealed Verdict

When verdicts come before examination, justice suffers.

When testimony is dismissed without review, truth becomes fragile.

And when questioning itself is treated as guilt, discernment becomes dangerous.

That is not how Scripture teaches us to handle accusation.

It is not how courts are meant to function.

And it is not how Christians should reason.

Why This Is the Greatest Lie

The greatest lie surrounding January 6 is not that something went wrong.

It's the claim that no questions were allowed because the truth was already known.

That lie did more than condemn a president.

It taught an entire generation that inquiry is disobedience,
that process is subversion,
and that truth must submit to consensus.

That is not justice.

That is control.

A Final Word on This Reason

You do not have to agree with Donald Trump's conclusions.

You do not have to share his instincts.

You do not have to defend his rhetoric.

But to say that asking questions made him the villain,
and that questioning itself justified permanent condemnation,
is neither honest nor just.

January 6 became the reason people say they hate Donald Trump
because it allowed them not to listen anymore.

And when listening stops, truth is no longer the goal.

What Christians Are Called to Do Instead

Christians are not called to slogans.
We are called to discernment.

We are not called to settle matters emotionally.
We are called to judge righteously.

And we are never called to trade truth for comfort,
no matter how loud the moment becomes.

That calling does not change with the headlines.

CONCLUSION:
A Call to Discernment

This book was never written to defend a man.

It was written to defend something far more fragile,
and far more important.

The way we reason.
The way we judge.
The way we decide what is true.

What This Book Was Really About

Every reason listed in these pages has one thing in common.

Each one relies on accusation being accepted without examination.

Labels replacing questions.
Narratives replacing process.
Emotion replacing discernment.

That pattern did not begin with Donald Trump, and it will not
end with him.

It is a temptation that appears in every generation, especially when fear
is high and certainty feels comforting.

Discernment Is Not Neutral

Discernment requires patience and courage.

It requires the willingness to slow down when everyone else is rushing to judgment.

It is much easier to repeat what we've heard than to test it.
Much easier to align with consensus than to examine evidence.
Much easier to stay quiet than to ask uncomfortable questions.

But ease has never been the measure of truth.

Why This Moment Matters

We are living in a time when accusation moves faster
than understanding.

When motives are assigned before facts are weighed.
When questioning is treated as defiance.
When disagreement is mistaken for disloyalty.

That environment does not produce justice.

It produces fear.

And fear is a poor foundation for truth.

What Christians Are Called to Be

Christians are not called to be reactionary.

We are called to be discerning.

That means we do not rush to judgment simply because a narrative is loud. We do not accept accusations simply because they are repeated. And we do not silence inquiry simply because it makes us uncomfortable.

Scripture teaches us to listen carefully, to judge righteously, and to refuse false witness — even when it costs us socially or politically.

That calling does not change when the stakes feel high.

A Final Charge

You do not have to agree with every conclusion in this book.

You do not have to share every concern raised in these pages.

But you should refuse to surrender your discernment.

Refuse to let accusation replace examination.
Refuse to let consensus replace truth.
Refuse to let fear do the work that discernment requires.

Because once discernment is abandoned, truth becomes optional.

And when truth becomes optional, justice cannot survive.

This is not a call to anger.
It is not a call to allegiance.

It is a call to discernment.

And that call belongs to every one of us.

POSTSCRIPT:
A Word About the Pattern

Let me say something that needs to be said, because this pattern keeps repeating.

Some things are tragic.
Truly tragic.

When a man dies and a family is shattered, we don't celebrate that. We don't excuse it. We don't minimize it.

But I'm not going to pretend we don't see what we're seeing.

The Double Standard Is the Tell

Here's the pattern.

If something happens to a Republican, or to someone connected to this president, the expectation is immediate.

You're supposed to speak like a pastor.
You're supposed to be gentle.
You're supposed to be careful.
You're supposed to act as if there was never any hatred aimed your way.

But let that same hatred be aimed *at the president*, and suddenly we're told it wasn't real.
Or it wasn't serious.
Or it doesn't count.

That's disingenuous.

And it's one of the clearest signs that something spiritual is happening in the way this man is judged.

Stop Requiring Him to Be Someone He Isn't

President Trump is not a pastor.

And I don't mean that as an insult. I mean it as reality.

People keep demanding that he behave like the man they *wish* he was, not the man he actually is. And when he refuses to play that role, they call it "beneath the office."

But watch what happens if he does speak with restraint.

If he says, "We're praying for you," people will say, "How could you bless someone who cursed you?"

If he says the obvious, people will say, "How dare you say it?"

So which is it?

The truth is, he's judged in a way other leaders are not judged.

And that's part of why the hatred grows — because the target is never allowed to be human.

A Personal Comment Isn't Automatically Political

Some things aren't "political statements."

They're personal.

And the way people twist every sentence into a headline is part of the machine. It's part of the pressure. It's part of the intimidation.

You can't threaten someone and then demand they pretend the threat never happened.

That isn't righteousness.
That isn't discernment.
That's manipulation.

The Surgeon Test

Let me put it plain.

If my child had a terminal illness, and the best surgeon in the country could save my child, but that surgeon was abrasive, rude, not religious, and did not fit my personal standards, I'm still choosing the best surgeon for the job.

Because in a crisis, what matters is effectiveness.

Our country has been battered.
Our communities have been shaken.
People are watching order collapse and pretending it's normal.

So the question becomes:

Are we actually evaluating outcomes?
Or are we punishing a man for not fitting a script?

Discernment Means Moral Consistency

As Christians, we are not called to protect any man from accountability.

But we are also not called to surrender our minds to outrage.

We are commanded to judge rightly.
We are warned not to accept a matter before hearing it fully.
We are cautioned against bearing false witness, not only by lying,
but by repeating things we haven't examined.

So here's my closing plea:

Don't let hatred do your thinking for you.
Don't let headlines train your conscience.
Don't let a cultural script replace moral clarity.

Because once discernment dies, anything can be justified as long
as the crowd agrees.

And that is not freedom.

That is not truth.

And that is not the mind of Christ.

Scripture Notes

Scripture references throughout this book are drawn
from commonly used English translations of the Bible.
In some instances, passages are paraphrased or referenced
for clarity and flow rather than quoted verbatim,
with care taken to remain faithful to the meaning of the text.

About the Author

Pastor Lorenzo Sewell is the senior pastor of 180 Church in Detroit, Michigan, where he leads with a focus on discipleship, discernment, and community transformation. His ministry is rooted in Scripture, pastoral care, and a commitment to engaging difficult cultural issues with clarity rather than outrage.

Raised in Detroit, Pastor Sewell has spent years serving in communities often overlooked by national conversations. His work has included mentoring, community advocacy, and pastoral leadership in environments shaped by economic pressure, political tension, and social fragmentation. These experiences have deeply informed his conviction that truth, process, and moral reasoning matter — especially when emotions run high.

Pastor Sewell is known for calling believers to think carefully, speak responsibly, and refuse the easy pull of slogans in place of discernment. He approaches public issues not as a partisan, but as a pastor concerned with how Christians reason, judge, and bear witness in the world.

He currently participates in national faith-based conversations through platforms such as FlashPoint, while remaining rooted in local church leadership and pastoral ministry.

He lives in Michigan with his wife and family and continues to serve the local church while engaging broader conversations about faith, truth, and responsibility in contemporary society.

More information about Pastor Sewell's ministry can be found at LorenzoSewell.com

www.ingramcontent.com/pod-product-compliance
Lightning Source LLC
Chambersburg PA
CBHW070254290326
41930CB00041B/2528